THE
INTOLERANT
'TOLERANT'
PARTY

Jarrad Shelton

The Intolerant, 'Tolerant' Party by Jarrad Shelton
Published by Lulu Press
3101 Hillsborough Street
Raleigh, NC 27607

http://www.lulu.com/

© 2014 Jarrad Shelton.
ISBN 978-1-387-26051-5

Cover by JD Griffin.

The Intolerant, 'Tolerant' Party

Jarrad Shelton

To my fellow Conservatives, keep up the good fight.

Contents

Forward   1

History of the Democratic Party   3

Andrew Jackson   9

Dred Scott   13

American Civil War   17

The Ku Klux Klan   21

Woodrow Wilson   23

Franklin Delano Roosevelt   25

Lyndon Johnson   27

Democratic Racism   31

The Modern Democratic Party   35

Afterword   39

References   41

Forward

Racist, sexist, extremist, naturalist, purist, sexist, bigot, homophobe, xenophobe, Nazi, white-supremacist, neocon, religious fanatic, and misogynist are just a few names I have been called simply for my Conservative beliefs. Not just me, but millions who share my beliefs. I knew what was in my heart and it was very frustrating being labeled something as vile as a racist. I believe most Conservatives don't have hate in their heart. Loving history and studying it all my life, I know who the party of racism was and still is, to some extent. I felt I need to write a book laying out who the party of racism and exclusion is exactly. The Democrats label themselves as the tolerant party all while practicing intolerance at the highest level. My book lays out facts, mixed with some personal beliefs and illustrates the racism that exists in this country and who was/is behind it. It is my sincere hope that you will find this book useful as you navigate the political world you live in.

Jarrad Shelton

History of the Democratic Party

The Democratic Party, believe it or not, was founded in the 1790's under the name Democratic-Republican. Thomas Jefferson, and James Madison, among others founded the party to oppose the Federalist Party, led by Alexander Hamilton & John Adams.

In 1828, Andrew Jackson is credited with founding the Democratic Party with which we are familiar today. The party was officially named Democrat in 1844. Jackson and his supporters were referred to as 'Jacksonian Democrats'. The 'Jacksonian Democracy' ended with the Civil War.

The Democrats held the Presidency all but two terms from 1828 to 1856. They lost only the 1840 election (William Henry Harrison defeated incumbent Martin Van Buren) and the 1848 (Zachary Taylor defeated Lewis Cass).

Leading up to the 1860 election, the Democratic Party was battling over the issue of slavery. The Southern Democrats, led by Jefferson Davis wanted to expand slavery to all the U.S. territories and the Northern Democrats, led by Stephan Douglas, wanted each individual territory to decide the issue for themselves. The Democrats lost the 1860 election, likely because of the split. The Southern Democrats nominated Vice President John Breckinridge of Kentucky, while the Northern Democrats nominated Stephan Douglas, Senator of Illinois.

Abraham Lincoln, candidate of the newly established anti-slavery Republican Party, narrowly won the 1860 election. Lincoln garnered some 40% of the national vote, Douglas 29% and Breckinridge won 18%. This election established the Democratic and the Republican Parties as the major parties in what was to become, a two-party system. This election was considered the first 'critical election' because it shaped the future of the country. Had the Democrats won, undoubtedly, slavery would have continued.

Following the Civil War, nationally, the Democrat Party was obsolete, only winning the Presidency twice when Grover Cleveland won in 1884 and again in 1892. The South remained a Democratic stronghold for nearly a century, as oppressive legislation and physical intimidation of newly freed African Americans ensured anyone who opposed Democratic beliefs would not vote.

The Democrat party split again in the 1896 election. This allowed William McKinley to win in a landslide over William Jennings Bryan. From 1896 to 1932, the Democrats only held the Presidency during the two terms of Woodrow Wilson (1913-1921). Many historians consider Wilson's first term a fluke. The Republican vote was split between incumbent William Howard Taft and former president Theodore Roosevelt, candidate of the Bull Moose Party.

In 1932, amidst the Great Depression, the Democrats won the Presidency as Franklin Roosevelt defeated President Herbert Hoover. Due to The Depression, the Democrats were able to not only win the Presidency, but replace the Republicans as the majority party in the United States House and Senate. Roosevelt would hold the Presidency from 1932-1944; breaking with the tradition set by George Washington, who would only run twice.

Harry Truman would become President following Roosevelt's death in 1945. Truman would narrowly defeat Thomas Dewey in 1948 to win the Presidency. The 1948 election is best known as the election where the Chicago Daily Tribune mistakenly ran the headline "Dewey Defeats Truman". The Democrats would be out of power until the election of 1960, where John F. Kennedy would narrowly defeat Richard Nixon.

From 1972 to 1988 the Democrats would lose 4 out of 5 Presidential elections. Richard Nixon would defeat Democrat Hubert Humphrey in 1968 to win the Presidency. The 1968 Democratic Convention was held in Chicago and was plagued by riots. No surprise that a city ran by Democrats for years would be the center of the riots. Following the Watergate Scandal and Richard Nixon's resignation, Governor Jimmy Carter's defeat of Gerald Ford was the lone victory. Plagued by a sluggish economy and the Iran Contra Affair, Carter would lose to Ronald Reagan in 1980.

The Democrats were out of power for the next three cycles until 1992 when Arkansas Governor Bill Clinton recaptured the White House. Clinton defeated President George H. W. Bush with the help of Texas Billionaire Ross Perot, who ran a 3rd party bid. Clinton would be re-elected in 1996, but would be plagued with scandal the rest of his presidency. Womanizer and misogynist, Bill Clinton had sex in the White House with a young intern named, Monica Lewinsky. He denied it for months, before finally confessing. In 1998, following a sexual harassment suit by Paula Jones, he was impeached by the House of Representatives for lying to Congress. Later, in 1999, not having enough votes for full impeachment, the Senate acquitted him. Accounts indicate the trial was nothing but a "dog and pony show". Using his expert legal skills he was able to parse words in the trial coining a phrase "It depends on what the meaning of 'is,' is. Unfortunately this became a joke following the trial. Vice President Al Gore was unable to win in 2000 losing to George W. Bush in a highly contested election that was finally settled by the Supreme Court.

The Democrats came back into power in 2008 as Barack Obama defeated John McCain. History has not been written on the Obama Presidency so I will not delve too deep into his Presidency. While in office, America ran up record debt, record number of people on food stamps, experienced the lowest number of people in the labor force, and the country became heavily divided along race, gender, and income lines. Obama played identity politics well. He turned the poor against the rich, black against white, and female against male. Twenty years from now, I believe people will look at his legacy and see a highly divisive man who believed America was an unjust country and believed it was his responsibility to right the perceived wrongs.

Andrew Jackson

Andrew Jackson was born on March 15, 1767 in the Waxhaws regions, an area geographically located on the border of North & South Carolina. He was a lawyer and rose to fame serving as a Major General in the War of 1812 before entering the House of Representatives and U.S.

The Hermitage

Senate representing Tennessee. He became a wealthy slave owner prior to being appointed Colonial of the Tennessee militia. Jackson owned as many as 300 slaves in his lifetime, working his plantation at Hermitage. Jackson had decisive victories in the War of 1812 defeating the British at the Battle of New Orleans making him a National Hero.

The War of 1812 brought America her National Anthem. The "Star Spangled Banner" was written by Francis Scott Key, originally penned as a poem. The words of "Defense of Fort M'Henry" were later put to music as lyrics and "Star Spangled Banner" was born. The lyrics were written to tell a story of the battle, - and had nothing to do with slavery; Key was inspired when he saw the American Flag flying at Fort McHenry. The "Star Spangled Banner" became our country's National Anthem on March 2, 1931.

Jackson ran for President in 1824, winning a plurality of the popular and Electoral votes. Since no candidate won a majority of the Electoral College, the House elected John Quincy Adams. Jackson ran again in 1828, winning in a landslide over Adams.

During Jackson's Presidency, his mistreatment of Native Americans was renowned. On May 28, 1830 Jackson signed the Indian Removal Act. The act relocated most Native American tribes in the South to Indian Territory. Jackson's mistreatment of Native Americans earned him the nickname "Indian Killer" or "Sharp Knife" by the Cherokee. Over 20,000 Native Americans died, -either directly or indirectly from the policies put in place by Jackson.

In his 8 years in office, Jackson signed about 70 treaties with Native Americans, -both in the South and the Northwest. Relationships between Indians and Americans became very tense and often times would become violent. While President, the Creek tribe lost 23 million acres of land in Southern Georgia and Central Alabama which; paved the way for future cotton plantations.

The Trail of Tears, while not happening under Jackson [Martin Van Buren], was the biggest genocide of Native Americans in our country's history. It was a direct result of Jackson's treatment of Native Americans. During the Trail of Tears, more than 45,000 Native Americans were relocated to the West. During the migration to the west, many Natives lost their lives to disease and starvation. The number is estimated at 15,000. The Cherokee, Muscogee, Seminole, Chickasaw, & Choctaw tribes were included in the relocation. The Cherokee lost the most members having 4000 deaths.

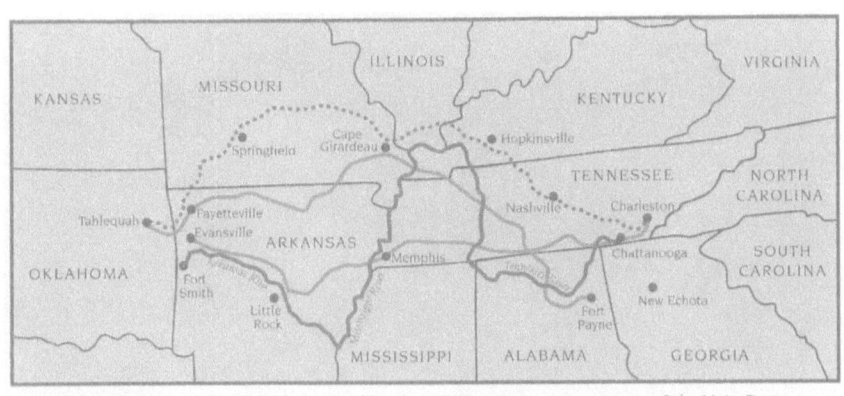

Trail of Tears National Historic Trail: ••••Land Route ━━Water Route ━━Other Major Routes

Dred Scott

Dred Scott vs. Sanford, known as the "Dred Scott Case", was decided on March 6, 1857. The Supreme Court stated that a "Negro" whose ancestors were imported to the U.S. and sold as slaves whether enslaved or free could not be American citizens and therefore had no standing to sue in Federal Court. The Federal government had no power to regulate slavery in the Federal territories acquired after the creation of the United States.

To better understand this case, you must first know the history of Dred Scott. Mr. Scott was born a slave in Virginia in 1795. His owner, Peter Blow, moved to Alabama in 1818 to work a farm near Huntsville. In 1830, Blow gave up farming and settled in Missouri where he sold Scott to Dr. John Emerson, an army surgeon. Emerson took Scott to Fort Armstrong in Illinois. Illinois was a "free state" and had prohibited slavery in its constitution in 1819 when it was admitted to the Union as a state.

In 1836, Emerson moved to Fort Snelling in the Wisconsin territory. Slavery was prohibited in this territory under the Missouri Compromise. While at Fort

Snelling, Scott married Harriet Robinson in a civil ceremony. Had Scott been a slave, the ceremony would have been unnecessary, as slave marriage had no recognition under the law.

By 1837, the army relocated Emerson to Jefferson Barracks Military Post, at Lemay, Missouri just south of St. Louis. Scott remained at Fort Snelling where he was leased out by Emerson. This essentially brought slavery to a free state, a direct violation of the law.

Shortly thereafter, the army reassigned Emerson to Fort Jessup in Louisiana. Here, Emerson married Eliza Irene Sanford in February1838. Emerson sent for Scott and his wife Harriet. While on the way to Louisiana, Scott's daughter Eliza was born on a steamboat between Illinois and what would later become Iowa. Since Eliza was born in a free territory, she was technically born a free person under federal and state law.

After Emerson died in 1843, his widow, Irene inherited his estate, including the slaves, the Scotts. In 1846, Scott attempted to purchase his family's freedom, but Irene Emerson refused forcing Scott to result in legal recourse.

The case went to the state's court where it was expected that the Scott family would win. Mr. Scott lost due to a technicality. During the trial a grocer, Samuel Russell, testified that he was leasing Scott from Irene Emerson, but later admitted that the arrangement had been made by his wife Adeline. Mr. Russell's testimony was ruled "hearsay" and the jury returned a verdict for Emerson.

In 1853, Scott sued again for his freedom. This time it took place in Federal court. At the trial in 1854, Judge Robert Wells directed the jury to rely on Missouri law to settle the question of Scott's freedom. Since the Missouri Supreme Court ruled that Scott remained a slave, the jury ruled in favor of Sanford. Scott appealed to the U.S. Supreme Court.

The Supreme Court ruled seven to two majority that Scott was not a citizen and had no standing to sue. Roger Taney was Chief Justice and was appointed by Andrew Jackson. The two dissenting voices were cast by Justice John McClean and Justice Benjamin R. Curtis.

American Civil War

The American Civil War was fought from 1861-1865. The war was a direct result of the fight over slavery and states' rights. The southern states that were run by Democratic governors wanted to allow slavery, while the northern states that were run by Republicans opposed slavery.

War broke out in April, 1861, shortly after Abraham Lincoln was inaugurated. The Confederate troops attacked Ft. Sumter in South Carolina, leading to war. This would continue for four years and was the deadliest war in American history leaving much of the South's infrastructure devastated. Approximately 750,000 soldiers were killed as a result of the Civil War.

In the 1860 election, Abraham Lincoln and other Republican Governors supported banning slavery in all the U.S. territories, while the Southern States wanted to expand slavery and viewed this as a violation of their Constitutional rights. As stated earlier, Lincoln would win the Presidency and become the first Republican to win the presidency. By the time Lincoln was inaugurated, seven "slave states" named themselves part of the Confederacy.

After Lincoln was elected, South Carolina called a State convention to consider succession. On December 20, 1860, South Carolina unanimously voted to secede from the Union. The "cotton states" of Mississippi, Florida,

The Battle of Antietam

Georgia, Alabama, Louisiana, and Texas would follow suit.

The states agreed to form a new government and on February 4, 1861 the Confederate States of America was formed. The Confederacy began seizing Federal forts and other land inside their borders.

The Civil War was known for the frequent and ferocious battles, usually resulting in massive casualties. During the war, 237 named battles were fought, mostly in the South. In1864, Lincoln made Ulysses S. Grant commander of the entire Union Army.

Grant, with help from William Tecumseh Sherman, who had been put in charge of the West, was able to turn the war around. On April 9, 1865, General Robert E. Lee, seeing the war had become hopeless, surrendered to Grant at Appomattox, Virginia.

The bloodiest war in United States history had come to an end. The root cause of the war is still up for debate; but there is no debate that slavery was one of the main issues. The Republicans wanted to end slavery altogether, the Democrats wanted to continue and grow slavery, leading to secession. Many Southern Governors had threatened secession if Lincoln won the 1860 election. After Lincoln won without carrying a single southern state, they felt secession was the only option. Southerners believed they no longer had representation and their ability to promote pro slavery policies would be heavily hindered.

The Ku Klux Klan

The Ku Klux Klan commonly referred to as the KKK, or simply the "Klan", was founded in Pulaski, Tennessee on December 24, 1865, during the reconstruction

The Ku Klux Klan on parade (D.C. 1928)

of the South after the Civil War. The Klan was formed by six Confederate veterans; Nathan Bedford Forrest became the Grand Wizard claiming to be the Klan's national leader.

Former Confederate General George Gordon

developed the Prescript which espoused white supremacist beliefs. He would often ask an applicant if he believed in a "white man's government", "the enfranchisement and emancipation of the white man in the south, and the restitution of Southern people to all their rights".

Klan members would wear all white robes and wear masks to hide their identities. Operating primarily at night, the Klan would attack blacks and other Southern Republicans, whom they saw as a threat. Klan members would work to suppress black voting, making campaign seasons deadly. There are many examples but a few include, - more than 2000 people being killed or wounded in Louisiana in the weeks before the 1868 Presidential election; despite a 1,071 Republican majority in St Landry Parrish, zero Republicans cast votes in that Parrish after the killings. In the 1868 Georgia gubernatorial election, Columbia County cast 1,222 votes for Republican Rufus Bullock. By the November presidential election, Klan intimidation had suppressed Republican vote to just 1 vote for Ulysses S. Grant.

By 1868, Klan activity was beginning to decrease. Many influential Southern Democrats feared that the Klan's lawlessness gave the North an excuse to take control in the South; therefore the leaders began to turn against them. The Klan remained a threat to African Americans for many years to come and still remains a dark stain on the fabric of our country's history.

Woodrow Wilson

Thomas Woodrow Wilson was born on December 28, 1856 and died on February 3, 1924. He was the first President to be elected from academia. Prior to entering politics he was President of Princeton University. To say Wilson was a racist, would be an understatement. While at Princeton he worked to discourage African Americans from applying.

Defeating incumbent Theodore Roosevelt, Wilson ran for President and became the 28th President of the United States. Wilson would become the first Progressive President, as his policies expanded government tremendously. Wilson continued his racism as President of U.S. While President, he segregated restrooms at Federal offices. At the Postal Service, African Americans were downgraded or even fired. Those who were not fired, were transferred to a different department and put behind screens where they would have no interactions with the public. Wilson opposed slavery, but not for a humanitarian reason. He saw it as wrong on economic grounds. In Wilson's 1901 book, A History of the American People, Wilson dismissed lynching committed by the Klan as a "lawless reaction to a lawless period". Thousands of blacks were drafted by the Army under Wilson. While they were given the same pay as whites they were kept in an all-black unit with white officers. When a group of black professionals protested discrimination Wilson replied "segregation is not a humiliation but a benefit, and ought to be so regarded by you gentlemen"[1].

Looking back on Wilson's Presidency, it is clear to see he was a racist man who saw African Americans as second class citizens.

Franklin Delano Roosevelt

Franklin Delano Roosevelt was born on January 30, 1882 and died April 12, 1945.

FDR is glorified as the biggest Progressive in the history of our country. When implemented, his New Deal programs moved us from a self-reliant country to a government dependent country. The New Deal programs were perceived as helping end the Great Depression but until we entered WWII in 1941, the economy was still weak, despite the massive debt incurred.

At his inauguration he began blaming the economic crisis on bankers and financiers, the quest for profits, and the self-interest of capitalism. Sound familiar to the rhetoric coming out of the Democratic Party today? He was an advocate of minimum wage. He said regarding minimum wage- "No business which depends for existence on paying less than living wages to its workers has any right to continue in this country"[2].

Roosevelt signed EO 9066, sending 120,000 Japanese expatriates and American citizens of Japanese ancestry to confinement at internment camps. The next time your Liberal friends accuse you of being racist because you support Donald Trump, ask them which Executive Order did President Trump sign that sent any group to internment camps?

Despite Jessie Owens winning 4 gold medals, as an African American in the 1936 Berlin Olympics, only white athletes were invited to the White House afterwards. Owens was offended, because he "wasn't invited to the White House to shake hands with the President"[3]. There is a widely believed myth that Hitler snubbed Owens at the Berlin games. However, Owens said, "Hitler didn't snub me; it was Roosevelt who snubbed me. The president didn't even send me a telegram"[4].

While Roosevelt saw lynching as murder, he would not support Republican proposals to make it a federal crime. He told an advocate: "If I come out for the anti-lynching bill now, they [Southern Democratic Senators] will block every bill I ask Congress to pass to keep America from collapsing; I just can't take that risk"[5].

FDR was no different than the Democratic Party today. Everything is politically motivated and there are no principals unless it will help you win politically.

Lyndon Johnson

Lyndon Baines Johnson, often referred to as LBJ, was born on August 27, 1908 in Stonewall, Texas and died January 22, 1973. He was America's 36th President, being sworn in following the assassination of John Kennedy in 1963.

Many people see LBJ as a civil rights hero; however he was a very racist man. This chapter will not be easy to read if you are easily offended. His "war on poverty" has led to the enslavement of many African Americans since its inception in 1964; a "war" we continue to fight today. In my humble opinion, we are losing the war with poverty, in part, by the policies put in place, by people like LBJ. Johnson's Great Society believed in expanding the Federal Governments role in education and healthcare to help reduce poverty. Johnson, being a Liberal, believed if we give up our freedoms to the Federal government, they could reduce or even prevent poverty in the U.S. Evidenced by his comment, "Our aim is not only to relieve the symptom of poverty, but to cure it and, above all, to prevent it"[6]. That is wonderful rhetoric, except that the government can't prevent poverty. In fact, more government intrusion leads to poverty. Policies like the Food Stamp Act of 1964 and the Social Security Act of 1965, have led to massive debt with little results. The Food Stamp Act, while well intended, has kept people in poverty. Many Americans see the lure of a handout from the government as too great to pass up. These policies were aimed at African Americans and were intentional. You will see the intentions later in this chapter.

Economist Milton Friedman argues that because of their interventionist nature, the policies had a negative impact. He said "the government sets out to eliminate poverty; it has a war on poverty, so-called 'poverty' increases. It has a welfare program, and the welfare program leads to an expansion of problems. A general attitude develops that government isn't a very efficient way of doing things."[7] Thomas Sowell, an American economist, social theorist, and author, also criticized the war on poverty stating "The black family, which had survived centuries of slavery and discrimination, began rapidly disintegrating in the Liberal welfare state; the subsidized unwed pregnancy and changed welfare from an emergency rescue to a way of life."[8] Here are the facts: African American "out of wedlock" births have risen from about 15%, prior to Johnson's war on poverty, to nearly 70% today. Regarding welfare, as of 2012, nearly 42% of African Americans were on welfare, the highest of any race. So, you can see the war on poverty is a war we are losing, and will continue to lose as long as government is interfering in Americans' lives.

While LBJ gets the credit for the 1964 Civil Rights Act, it was actually submitted to Congress in June of 1963, by JFK. Johnson would often refer to the bill as the "nigger bill". After numerous debates and Democratic filibusters, the bill passed and was signed into law on July 2, 1964. The Civil Rights Act is a good thing and it is wonderful that Johnson signed it, but one should look at the motives before praising Johnson. According to Ronald Macmillan, a former Air Force One steward, Johnson was explaining to a group of Democratic governors why the Civil Rights Bill was so important to him Johnson said: "I'll have those niggers voting Democratic for the next two hundred years."[9] It was not done out of equality for everyone, rather a ploy for the Democratic Party.

As stated earlier, Johnson was a racist. According to Simeon Booker, a long time Jet correspondent, Johnson lectured Booker after a critical article telling Booker he should "thank" Johnson for all he'd done for black people. Johnson's biographer Robert Dallek writes in Flawed Giant that Johnson explained his decision to nominate Thurgood Marshall to the Supreme Court rather than a less famous black judge by saying "When I appoint a nigger to the bench, I want everybody to know he is a nigger".[10] According to Robert Parker, who was Johnson's chauffeur, there was a moment where Johnson asked Parker whether he would prefer to be referred to by his name, rather than "boy", "nigger", or "chief". When Parker said he would, Johnson became angry saying "As long as you are black, and you're going to be black till the day you die, no one's going to call you by your goddamn name. So, no matter what you are called, 'nigger', you just let it roll off your back like water, and you'll make it. Just pretend you're a goddamn piece of furniture."[10]

Johnson believed that African Americans could not function in society without help from the government. He created plans, not out of the goodness of his heart, rather for political motivation. As you take a closer look at Johnson's life and his beliefs, it becomes clear he was closer to a racist than a civil rights hero.

Democratic Racism

In This chapter I will focus on events in history that were perpetrated by the Democrats. I will also take a look at racist Democratic leaders of the past.

The Jim Crow laws were state and local laws that enforced racial segregation in the South. The laws were put in place by Democrat State legislatures in the late 19th century. They mandated segregation in all public places. Contrary to some beliefs, Jim Crow was not a person. "Jim Crow" was a derogatory term meaning "Negro". Schools, bathrooms, and railroad cars were all segregated. The motto "separate but equal" was the basis for the segregation. As stated earlier, Woodrow Wilson even got in on the act, segregating Federal workplaces. "Separate but equal" was a terrible phrase, and equal it certainly wasn't. The "colored" only spaces were substandard and often underfunded. One example-a "white man's" bathroom might be cleaned every day; a "colored man's" bathroom would be filthy, rarely ever cleaned.

The Declaration of Constitutional Principles, known informally as the Southern Manifesto, was written in

1956. It opposed racial integration in public places. It was signed by 101 politicians, mostly Democrats (99). Several prominent leaders signed it. William Fulbright and John McClellan from my home state of Arkansas signed it. Strom Thurmond, Senator from South Carolina, was the most notable person to sign it. At that time Strom Thurmond was one of the most powerful Senators and when opposing the Civil Rights Bill of 1957, he staged an 24 hour and 18 minutes, nonstop filibuster; the longest ever by a single Senator. It is worth noting that in 1964, he had a change of heart and switched to the Republican Party.

Robert Byrd was a U.S. Senator from West Virginia. Mr. Byrd was also a member of the KKK prior to joining the Senate. Byrd held the highest position in the Klan, the Exalted Cyclops. Byrd opposed the Civil Rights Act of 1964; when he was in the Senate he personally held a filibuster of the bill for 14 hours. Byrd was also the mentor of 2016 Democratic Presidential Candidate Hillary Clinton.

George Wallace was the longtime Democratic governor of Alabama. Wallace passionately believed in segregation. He announced in 1963 he believed in "segregation now, segregation tomorrow, segregation forever"[11]. Governor Wallace stood at the entrance of the University of Alabama to oppose Vivian Malone and James Hood, the first two African Americans enrolled, from entering the school. With help from, Birmingham's Commissioner of Public Safety, Bull Conner, he treated African Americans like garbage. Bull Conner would often use his attack dogs and water hoses on innocent black people of Alabama.

Orval Faubus was Democratic Governor of Arkansas from 1955 to 1967. While Governor, he ordered the National Guard to prevent black students from entering Little Rock Central High School. The "Little Rock Nine" as it became to be known was a direct violation of Brown vs Board of Education. Republican President, Dwight D. Eisenhower intervened bringing the matter to an end.

Margaret Sanger, to the Democratic Party, is a hero. Sanger opened the first birth control clinic in America. She established organizations that would become Planned Parenthood.

Margaret Sanger is nothing but a racist. She established her clinics for the sterilization of vulnerable people, including people she considered "feeble-minded", "idiots", and "morons". Most of her clinics were set up in poor, mostly minority neighborhoods.

She spoke at a KKK rally in 1926. In a 1939 letter to Clarence Gable, she wrote "We do not want word to go out that we want to exterminate the Negro population, and the minister is the man who can straighten out the idea if it ever occurs to any of their more rebellious members"[12]. How appalling is that? And this is the woman the left looks up to as a hero!

Margaret Sanger believed in population control through birth control. She believed in eliminating the weaker people in hopes of creating a super class of citizens.

She saw African Americans problems to society, which is why she established most of her clinics in the minority community. Her clinics transformed into Planned Parenthood which is nothing but an abortion factory. They are the leaders in the abortion industry, mostly done on African Americans, at nearly 40%.

Margaret Sanger set out to eliminate African Americans and Planned Parenthood is living up to her expectations.

The Modern Democratic Party

The Democratic Party of today is as radical as it has ever been. The leaders of the party, folks like: Barack Obama, Hillary Clinton, Bernie Sanders, Elizabeth Warren, Chuck Schumer, & Nancy Pelosi are trying to take the party so far left, close to socialism, that they have virtually eliminated all the moderates from the party.

They are no longer the party of the working class, people I believe they look down their noses at. They are the party of the elites- Hollywood, academic, etc., and the party of the poor. Hollywood funds their pursuit of election so they can create more laws, which raise taxes, so they can fund the government run programs, aimed at buying votes of the poor. The rich don't mind their taxes being raised because they can afford the best lawyers and accountants to find loopholes. Meanwhile, the middle-class can't get a break. When our taxes go up, we can't afford a great law firm to help, so we just skip a vacation or take a second job. It's not fair, but the Democrats are not about fairness, they are about power!

Programs like the Affordable Health Care Act

(Obamacare), food stamps, Section 8 housing, Medicaid, just to name a few, while well intended, have had the reverse effect. Obamacare was a fraud rammed down our throats with zero Republican support. Labeled Affordable, it is a joke. The plan has totally been a failure. Premiums have risen tremendously as a result of the ACA. Many more people lost their coverage as a result of the plan. It never would have passed if not for the "Cornhusker Kickback". Nevada Senator Harry Reid had to offer $100 million in Medicaid funding to Senator Ben Nelson of Nebraska to get him to vote yes. The plan was so bad that not only did they have to buy votes through the "Cornhusker Kickback", but they had to put a provision in the bill called the individual mandate to insure Americans would buy it. If the bill was so great, wouldn't Americans want to buy it? It wasn't, they knew it wasn't, that's why they insisted on the individual mandate. The Democrats didn't care; it was a social justice play and a redistribution of wealth.

The Democratic Party of today is obsessed with race. Every issue revolves around race with them. If you oppose these wonderful programs, you must be a racist. Perhaps, we simply want to cut the fraud and abuse, but that can't be the case according to the Democrats.

The Democrats are the true racists because, like LBJ, they believe African Americans could never survive without government. They proclaim if we do away with affirmative action, blacks and other minorities will not be able to get into college or be able to get a job. Now that's racism; they are essentially saying without government leveling the playing field, you can't succeed. Never mind your talents or skill, you need government help.

The Democrats keep poor and minorities in sub-standard housing through Section 8 housing. They provide government housing in the worst neighborhoods, many filled with crime and drugs. They set the standards so you can earn enough money to get by, but not to get ahead. From speaking to people who live in government housing, the people tell me "they want to get out, but can't". They say they can't because if they take a better job so they can afford to move, they will lose their assistance.

The Democrat Party knows exactly what they are doing. They create government plans intended to help the poor. They put enough restrictions on the plans to keep you poor. Then they show up every 2 or 4 years asking for your vote. They are quick to point out what they have done, rather than point out who it has actually helped.

The Democrat Party lectures everyone about how tolerant they are and call us intolerant but let's look at the facts. The Democrats are only tolerant if you have the same beliefs as they do.

On several key issues they hold a one sided view, and if you oppose you have to be a racist or one of many other degrading names. Regarding speech, they claim to be for the 1st amendment yet they will shut down a college campus anytime a Conservative comes to speak.

Through groups like Antifa, they will shut down, using violence any speech they deem 'hate speech'. If you oppose same-sex marriage, they claim you are a homophobe and should be questioned by the police. The Democrats have used the legal system to force a private owner to do what they believe is right regarding bakers making cakes for a same-sex marriage. The Democrats believe in using force to get what they want rather than just accepting other people's opinions. This is the "intolerance" from the "tolerant" party.

Afterword

I, in no way, am implying that all Democrats are racist. That was never the intention of this book. The purpose of the book was to point out the racist history of the Democrat Party, through facts. The Democrats want to erase history by tearing down statues all the while they are the cause of America's racist past. Perhaps if we can have honest dialogue without being so quick to label someone, we can advance the real issues. I do believe racism still exists today, but it is not rampant as the left want to portray. The Democrats benefit through fear. The media, which is an extension of the Democratic Party, makes every issue about race, trying to divide America. The intention, I believe is to create fear in hopes that people look to government for help, thus increasing their powers.

References

1. Barnett, R. (2015, June 25). Expunging Wood-row Wilson from Official Places of Honor. Re-trieved from https://www.washingtonpost.com/news/volokh-conspiracy/wp/2015/06/25/expung-ing-woodrow-wilson-from-official-places-of-honor/

2. Tritch, T. (2014, March 07). F.D.R. Makes the Case for the Minimum Wage. Retrieved from https://tak-ingnote.blogs.nytimes.com/2014/03/07/f-d-r-makes-the-case-for-the-minimum-wage/

3. Schwartz, L. (2005). Owens pierced a myth. Re-trieved from https://espn.go.com/sportscentury/fea-tures/00016393.html

4. Schaap, J. (2008). *Triumph: The Untold Story of Jesse Owens and Hitler's Olympics*. Boston: Mariner Books.

5. Beasley, M. H., Shulman, H. C., & Beasley, H. R. (2001). *The Eleanor Roosevelt Encyclopedia*. West-port, CT: Greenwood Press.

6. Matthews, D. (2014, January 08). Everything you need to know about the war on poverty. Retrieved from https://www.washingtonpost.com/news/wonk/wp/2014/01/08/everything-you-need-to-know-about-the-war-on-poverty/

7. Milton Friedman Interview. (2002, August 9). Retrieved from http://www.pbs.org/fmc/interviews/friedman.htm

8. Sowell, T. (2004, August 17). Thomas Sowell - A painful anniversary. Retrieved from https://townhall.com/columnists/thomassowell/2004/08/17/a-painful-anniversary-n1190382

9. Kessler, R. (1995). *Inside the White House: The Hidden Lives of the Modern Presidents and the Secrets of the World's Most Powerful Institution.* New York: Pocket Books.

10. Serwer, A. (2014, April 12). Lyndon Johnson was a civil rights hero. But also a racist. Retrieved from http://www.msnbc.com/msnbc/lyndon-johnson-civil-rights-racism

11. Richman, J., Freemark, S., & Shapiro, B. (2013, January 10). 'Segregation Forever': A Fiery Pledge Forgiven, But Not Forgotten. Retrieved from http://w Time.com / Jennifer Latson ww.npr.org/2013/01/14/169080969/segregation-forever-a-fiery-pledge-forgiven-but-not-forgotten

12. Latson, J. (2016, October 14). Margaret Sanger, Race and Eugenics: A Complicated History. Retrieved from http://time.com/4081760/margaret-sanger-history-eugenics/